Get Wise

Right or Wrong

⇒ what difference does it make?

Sarah Medina

Heinemann

www.heinemann.co.uk/library

Visit our website to find out more information about **Heinemann Library** books.

To order:

☎ Phone 44 (0) 1865 888066

📄 Send a fax to 44 (0) 1865 314091

💻 Visit the Heinemann Bookshop at www.heinemann.co.uk/library to browse our catalogue and order online.

First published in Great Britain by Heinemann Library, Halley Court, Jordan Hill, Oxford OX2 8EJ, part of Harcourt Education.

Heinemann is a registered trademark of Harcourt Education Ltd.

Editorial: Lucy Thunder and Helen Cannons
Design: David Poole and Kamae Design
Illustrations: Jeff Anderson
Picture Research: Rebecca Sodergren and Kay Altwegg
Production: Edward Moore

Originated by Repro Multi-Warna
Printed and bound in China by WKT Company Limited

The paper used to print this book comes from sustainable resources.

ISBN 0 431 21000 4 (hardback)
08 07 06 05
10 9 8 7 6 5 4 3

ISBN 0 431 21006 3 (paperback)
09 08 07 06 05
10 9 8 7 6 5 4 3 2 1

British Library Cataloguing in Publication Data
Medina, Sarah
Right or wrong – what difference does it make?. – (Get wise)
170
A full catalogue record for this book is available from the British Library.

Acknowledgements
The Publishers would like to thank the following for permission to reproduce photographs: Alamy Images p.**5**, **17**, **24**; ARDEA p.**21**; Corbis/RF p.**15**, /Tom and Dee Ann McCarthy p.**14**; FPLA pp.**7**, **23**; Bubbles p.**11**; Getty/Tony Stone Images p.**12**; Sally and Richard Greenhill pp.**13**, **18**, **29**; National Association of Clubs for Young People p.**19**; Panos Pictures p.**25**; Photofusion/Paul Baldesare p.**16**, /Robert Brook p.**22**, /Jacky Chapman p.**9**, /Brian Mitchell p.**4**, /Maggie Murray p.**26**, /Roderick Smith p.**9**, /David Tothill p.**6**.

Cover photograph of graffiti on wall, reproduced with permission of Photofusion/Graham Burns.

Quotes and news items are taken from a variety of sources, including BBC News, BBCi Newsround and the United Nations Pachamama website.

The Publishers would like to thank Glynnis Hendra, Advisory Teacher for PSHE and Citizenship, for her assistance in the preparation of this book.

Every effort has been made to contact copyright holders of any material reproduced in this book. Any omissions will be rectified in subsequent printings if notice is given to the Publishers.

Contents

Words appearing in bold, **like this**, are explained in the Glossary.

Every day – almost every moment – we make decisions. How do we know what is right and what is wrong?

What shall I wear this morning? Which book, magazine or TV programme do I want to enjoy next? What do I think about this – or that? Most of the decisions we make are fairly simple. Some are trickier, and we have to think about them more. Some are very hard, involving difficult choices between right and wrong.

Right or wrong?

We all know that some things are completely right – even if we find them hard to stick to. We know that it is right to be kind to other people and to animals, for example. It is also right to look after the **environment**. Some things are very clearly wrong, too. We know that we should not hurt or bully other people. Stealing and **vandalism** are also wrong. Rules and **laws** often tell us what is right or wrong.

Leaving others out just because you think they don't 'fit' is hurtful. How do you think this person feels? Next time, do the right thing – ask them to join in with you!

Or not so sure?

Sometimes, it can be harder to know exactly what is right or wrong. People can have different opinions about the same thing. For example, **vegetarians** choose not to eat meat because they believe that it is cruel to animals. But other people say that you can eat meat and still be kind to animals.

Getting it right

We all live together – at home and school, in our community and the world. Everything we do has an effect on somebody or something else. If you throw litter on the street, it will have a bad effect: someone will have to clean up after you. If you help someone who is unhappy, it will have a good effect: they – and you – will feel happier. Getting it right means trying to do the right thing whenever you can.

Talk time

When do you have to think about right and wrong in your day-to-day life?

 Lauren: Well, you might have to choose whether to do everything your friends do.

ali: Yeah, especially if they're doing stuff you don't like, like smoking.

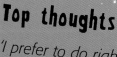

Tyrone: And at home, sometimes it's hard to get on with people. They can really wind you up!

Maribel: Yeah! And do you really have to do everything you are told?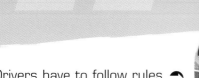

Drivers have to follow rules ➜ that tell them the right things to do on the road – otherwise, there would be crashes all the time!

Are some things definitely always right or wrong?

Some people have very set ideas about right and wrong. They have what is sometimes called a 'black and white' view. For example, they may believe that people should always tell the truth (this is 'white', or right), and that lying is never acceptable (it is 'black', or wrong). They always keep to their view, even if it means that they – or someone else – may get into trouble.

🔊 Rules can keep people safe. Cyclists who follow the rules and signal carefully before turning or stopping help to prevent accidents.

Talk time

Is lying always wrong?

ali: Yes – lying is really bad. If you lie to people, you hide things from them and you don't care about them very much. Then, if they find out, they stop trusting you.

Maribel: Yeah, and lying can get out of control. You start with one lie, then tell another lie to hide the first one – and so on. After a while, you feel really bad about yourself.

Lauren: White lies aren't so bad, are they? If someone asked you if they looked nice, and they didn't – you wouldn't tell them that, would you?

Tyrone: Probably not! But it's still better to tell the truth whenever you can.

Getting it right?

Think about stealing for a minute. Some people say that stealing is always wrong. Other people say that – if you live in a really poor country and you are starving – stealing some food to eat is not so wrong. It can get quite confusing! So how do people know what to do? Rules can help us to understand what is right and what is wrong.

Rules rule OK!

Rules are a kind of guideline about right and wrong, and they help us to make the right choices. Some rules help people to stay safe. The Cycling Proficiency Scheme teaches children rules about using bikes safely – for example, you should always keep both hands on the handlebars unless you are signalling or changing gear. These rules are 'black and white' – if you do the right thing, you will stay safe, but if you do the wrong thing, you may hurt yourself or other people. Rules at home, school and in the community also help us to live and work together – because they show us the right way to treat others.

❶ It is always wrong to steal, even from animals. Birds that are risk of dying out, like this peregrine falcon, are the target of people who steal eggs for their collections.

THINK IT THROUGH

Do rules help us to know about right and wrong?

Yes. If there weren't any rules, no one would really know if something was right or wrong. It would be just up to each person to decide for themselves.

No. Rules change all the time. Some schools have some rules and others have different ones – so who's to say what's right?

What do YOU think?

What do laws tell us about right and wrong?

Have you ever been tempted to take something from a shop without paying? Do you know anyone who has done it? This is shoplifting. It is a crime and it is against the **law**. Like all crimes, it is wrong. There are many other crimes, including stealing and violence. All countries have laws that set out what is right and wrong. Laws make it clear which actions are crimes, and help to protect us from people who break the law.

The consequences of crime

All crimes have **consequences**. If you have had something stolen – maybe a scooter or bike – you will probably feel really upset. You may have lost something that was a special gift. It may have been expensive, and you may have to wait a long time to have it replaced. You may worry that you will have something else stolen in the future.

Crimes against property – for example, **vandalism** – often affect not just one person, but a whole community. Everyone has the right to enjoy public areas, such as parks. It is hard to enjoy them if vandals break things, leave chewing gum and litter lying around, or write graffiti everywhere. This sort of damage can make people feel unsafe. And someone will have to pay to clean up the mess.

Vandalism spoils ➲ the community for everyone, and makes people feel worried about going out or about about their safety.

Crime and punishment

People who break the law are usually punished. If the person who committed the crime is caught, they may have to go to **court**. A **judge** or **magistrates** will then decide on a punishment – for example, paying some money (a fine) or doing work to help the community. In serious cases, the person may go to prison.

Newsflash

A teenage girl who committed 125 crimes over 2 years has been banned from her local town centre for 5 years. Previous attempts to stop her from breaking the law failed. The teenager will go to prison for up to two years if she disobeys the ban.

The police work to prevent crime – and to educate young people about staying out of trouble.

How can you decide if something is right or wrong if there are no rules or **laws** about it?

Many people believe that the right or wrong thing to do depends on the situation. Different people may have different opinions about what is right. Even so, most people do stick to certain standards about right and wrong, which are generally accepted by most people in their country.

Me, me, me!

Some people are selfish, and always put their own needs first. Perhaps they forget to take their pencil case to school. They don't have time to go home to fetch it, and they don't want to ask the teacher to borrow what they need, in case they get into trouble. Their friends don't have any spare pens. And so they simply decide to steal someone else's pencil case. They do not stop to think about how that other person will feel. As long as they have what they want, they are happy – even if they make other people unhappy.

Top thoughts

'It is the greatest good to the greatest number of people which is the measure of right and wrong.'

Jeremy Bentham,
English thinker
(1748–1832)

Me ... and you

Other people believe that we should think about other people as well as ourselves. We should be prepared to put ourselves out for others. Perhaps you could help your sister with her homework or do the washing up, even if you want to go out with your friends. By helping others, you are doing the right thing – and you make the world a much nicer place to live in!

❶ Helping an older friend or relative with their shopping may be time consuming – but it helps them a lot, and it is the right thing to do.

TOP TIPS

Your friends are smoking, and they want you to try, too. You don't really want to – so what do you do? If you say no, they might stop talking to you. If you say yes, you go against your own feelings, and you put your health at risk. Follow these top tips to make the right choice – whatever the circumstances:

◎ First, pause for a minute.

◎ Think about the different choices you could make.

◎ Think about the consequences of these choices.

◎ Think about the good and bad things about each choice.

◎ Now go ahead with making your choice.

THINK IT THROUGH

Should people always put themselves first?

Yes. We have to look out for ourselves, because no one else will.

No. We have to think about other people, too, because we don't just live on our own.

What do **YOU** think?

Is what we think about right and wrong influenced by other people?

As we grow up, we learn about right and wrong from lots of different people, including our parents, teachers and friends. We also learn different views about what is right and wrong from TV, radio, newspapers and magazines.

Peer and media pressure

Peer pressure is when your friends or family try to get you to do something you might not do otherwise. Media pressure is when newspapers, magazines, TV and radio programmes and advertisements influence your choices because they put across very strong views, or views that seem to be 'normal'.

Think about your favourite soap opera on TV. Does it show people lying to each other? Do you think that this is normal and right? Does it make your life easier if you sometimes lie to people you know? And if your friends do something you know is wrong, do you always join in with them? Stop for a minute and think about how much your choices are affected by outside pressures like these.

Newsflash

Advertising can have a big influence on the choices people make. Some people believe that adverts for junk food should be banned. The Food Commission – which checks up on people's eating habits in the UK – says that children are suffering because they are so unhealthy. They blame this on food and drink companies targeting young people with their adverts. They found that of 358 foods marketed to young people, 77 per cent had high levels of unhealthy sugar, salt or fat.

↻ Companies spend millions of pounds on advertising because they know they can persuade people to buy their products.

Talk time

How can you stand up to negative peer pressure to do something that is wrong?

 ali: It helps if you know your own opinions about things. You have to trust them, too.

Maribel: Yeah. I'd never start smoking for example – it's just stupid. It can kill you!

 Lauren: If your friends think the same as you, that helps. You should be careful who you hang out with!

Tyrone: It's good if you can talk to someone about stuff, too. If you can talk to a friend, that's great. Or you could talk to an adult, too – like your mum or dad, or a teacher – if you think you're being pushed into something.

🎧 If you have been told not to go somewhere, would you do it just because your friends do? Get it right: make up your own mind!

THINK IT THROUGH

Is peer pressure good or bad?

Good. If other people didn't tell us their views, we would never learn anything at all.

Bad. Some people get into all sorts of trouble because they do what others say and ignore their own opinions.

Good and bad! Peer pressure can help you to do the right thing, but sometimes it can push you into wrong choices.

What do YOU think?

How do you do the right thing in the hustle and bustle of family life?

Top thoughts

'Having a family is like having a bowling alley installed in your head.'

Martin Mull, actor

➲ Patience, respect and co-operation help families to live together happily.

D o you live with one parent or carer, or two – or do you split your time between them? Do you have brothers and sisters? Do you have a step-parent and a step-family? Nowadays, family life can be quite complicated. It can also be very challenging, as we learn to live together in the best way possible.

Getting mad – and sad

Sometimes we treat the people we love most the worst. It's easy to shout at your mum or brother, because you know they're going to stick around – and, anyway, you'll make up eventually. It is easy to get things wrong in the family. We fight about who does what, who has what, and even who loves who the most! All this does is make everyone unhappy. It's just not worth it.

Sharing and caring

Everyone in the family has **rights** and responsibilities. This means that there are things you can expect for yourself – but also things you should do for others. You have the right to be loved and looked after, and to be given more responsibility as you grow up. The people who care for you have the right to be respected and listened to, and for you to help them. Everyone shares responsibilities, too: to be honest and fair, and to listen to each other's views. Everybody makes mistakes. We all should expect to be forgiven for getting things wrong, and we should also forgive others who make mistakes.

We all have rights and responsibilities. As you get older, you have the right to be given more freedom. You have responsibility to let your family know where you are going and when you are coming home.

TOP TIPS

These tips will to help you get along with your family:

- ◎ Remember your rights – and your responsibilities!
- ◎ Respect each other's space – knock before going into someone's room.
- ◎ Respect each other's things – ask permission before borrowing anything.
- ◎ People can't read your mind – so tell them what you think, feel and need!
- ◎ Think ahead – how will what you do make someone else feel?
- ◎ Have a laugh – sharing fun makes family life much easier.
- ◎ Keep talking – and listening!

THINK IT THROUGH

Should adults and children share the jobs around the house?

No. Adults should do the jobs, because they're the ones who want them done.

Yes. Everyone should share the boring jobs. After all, everyone wants to share the fun stuff!

What do YOU think?

How do you do what is best at school?

When you are at school, you have to deal with many different people and situations – with friends and teachers, lessons and break times. School rules make some choices very clear – but you will have to make other choices about right and wrong for yourself.

Messing up

What do you think about school? Is it just something that gets in the way of your fun? Some people have this attitude, and they start doing the wrong things. They may mess around in class, which makes it hard for other people to learn. They may start bullying other people. These choices make it really hard for them and others to get on at school.

Doing the right thing can seem boring. Homework may take time, but it will help you to learn more and to become more confident.

Talk time

Why is bullying wrong?

Tyrone: Well, it hurts people a lot.

Lauren: Yeah, and not just physically. Bullying makes people feel really miserable.

Maribel: You can get really scared if someone's after you.

ali: Bullying's bad for the bully, too. They must have problems if they have to bully other people to feel good.

Lauren: Yes – maybe they feel that they are no good at school or something.

Maribel: Maybe. But it's still no excuse. Bullying is just wrong.

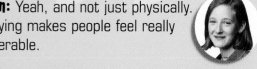

Doing your best

You can get the best out of school by making the right choices. If you talk and listen to other people, you will soon become friends – and you will have more fun. If you look after the school grounds, you will have a pleasant **environment** to work in and enjoy. Doing your homework means that you will learn more.

Get up and go!

You can help the school to do what is right, too – in the rules and decisions that it makes. Get involved as much as you can. You could try being part of a **school council**. You could put ideas into a suggestion box, or discuss your views in class.

THINK IT THROUGH

Is school cool?

Yes. School's a great place to learn about the world. You get to hang out with friends, too.

No. School's boring. It's just another place where people tell you what to do.

What do YOU think?

Newsflash

It is important for students to like and trust their teachers. A group of children at a London school have been allowed to help interview the people who want to be their new headteacher. Students Nathan and Leo said: 'We think that children should get to interview teachers, because children will get a chance to find out more about the teacher, and to also know how they treat children.'

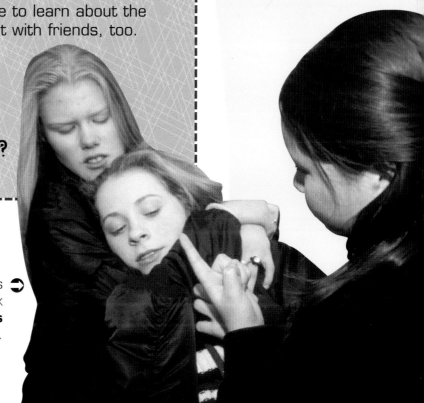

Bullying hurts. Bullies ➲ should stop to think about the **consequences** of their actions.

How can we make living in our community better?

Fact Flash

Fact Flash

In 2002, **vandalism** to UK payphones cost £4 million.

Your community is the place you live in. Different communities have different facilities, such as shops and schools, youth clubs, sports centres and parks. They also have lots of different people – young and old. When you live in a community, you get to know the places and people there – and this makes it feel like home.

Opting out

Is there litter on your streets? Are the swings broken in your park? Are the windows smashed in your youth club? People who damage their community spoil things – for other people, and for themselves, too. If you don't care about your community, you can feel as if you don't belong.

⊙ By picking up rubbish, these people are making their community a much nicer place to live in.

Joining in

If you care about your community, you will help to make it a better place. Joining in with activities, such as Cubs or Scouts, Brownies or Guides, or theatre, music and sports, is great fun and really makes you feel part of things. Keeping your community clean and tidy makes you feel proud of where you live. Helping other people whenever you can will make everyone feel good. You can even get involved in decisions about how to run your community. Try writing to your **local council** to suggest ideas for things you think your community needs, such as a skatepark. You could also help with **fundraising** for community projects.

Taking part in community activities, such as this youth club, is fun and brings people together. It is far better than hanging around on street corners with nothing to do.

THINK IT THROUGH

Are communities important?

No. The only thing that matters is my friends. The community has nothing to do with me.

Yes. We all belong to a community. And the more you put into it, the more you get out of it.

What do YOU think?

What is the right way to treat animals?

There are animals all around us: wild animals, such as squirrels and hedgehogs; farm animals, such as cows and sheep; and our favourites – our family pets! All animals have needs. Just like people, they need food, water and exercise, and a safe place to live. The way we treat animals can be right or wrong.

Just for us?

Do you think that animals are less important than humans? If you see an insect, do you just stamp on it? If you have a pet, do you sometimes forget to look after it? Some people either ignore animals, or think that animals are just there for us to use – for sport, entertainment or food, or even for testing products, such as medicines, and even **cosmetics**. This way of treating animls is wrong.

Ah, nothing. It was only a human!

Oop! What was that?

Or our equals?

Many people believe that animals are our equals. They look after their pets as if they were loved and respected members of their family. They refuse to hunt or catch animals for sport. Some choose to be **vegetarian** or, if they do eat meat, they try to make sure that the animals do not suffer.

Most countries have **laws** to prevent animal suffering. And many organizations, such as the Royal Society for the Prevention of Cruelty to Animals (RSPCA) and Animals Australia, also work to protect animals. You can **volunteer** to help them with this work, too.

TOP TIPS

Follow these top tips for caring for your pet!

◎ Spend some quality time with your pet every day.

◎ Make sure it has the healthy food it needs, and lots of fresh water.

◎ Give it plenty of exercise – and a cosy place to sleep when it is tired!

◎ Always take your pet to the vet if it is hurt or unwell.

Dogs need a daily walk to keep fit and healthy. You can help your dog and have fun with it at the same time!

THINK IT THROUGH

Is it wrong to use animals for testing products?

Yes. Animals have feelings, just like us, and they shouldn't be used to test products, because it might hurt them.

No. By testing products on animals, people make sure that they are safe for humans, too.

Sometimes. It is wrong to test cosmetics on animals, but it is OK to use animals to test really important products, such as medicines.

What do YOU think?

What should we do to look after our world properly?

Top thoughts

'Inside every big issue are hundreds of little issues that may do more damage to the environment than the big one.'

Jukka Uosukainen, government minister, Finland

Our home, the Earth, looks after us well. It provides us with everything we need. How well do you think we look after the Earth? You may not think it, but the choices we make each day can have a really big impact on the whole world. Even little things, such as leaving lights on or dropping litter, affect our **environment**. And so we need to be careful to make the right choices.

Being greedy

Humans have always used nature for food, water and shelter. This is OK, but in recent years we have become too greedy. Some of our choices are causing nature to be 'used up'.

In countries such as the UK, the USA and Australia, we like to live comfortably. By doing whatever we please and buying as much as we want, we create a lot of rubbish and **pollution** and we waste a lot of water. This is wrong, because it damages the environment – and it means that life will be harder for people in the future.

Dropping litter is wrong. It can end up polluting our rivers and the sea, killing fish and other animals. It looks ugly, too.

Taking care

Many people try very hard to take care of the Earth. There is lots that you can do, too. Instead of throwing paper, card, glass, aluminium or clothing in the bin, why don't you **recycle** it? This means that new things can be made from your old rubbish! Remember to switch off lights and the TV when you are not using them, too. And you could get involved with organizations, such as Friends of the Earth and Greenpeace, that work to protect the environment (see page 31).

By collecting and using rain water to ➲ water the plants at home or school we use less tap water. That way, we help the environment.

(see page 31)

THINK IT THROUGH

Do we really need to look after the Earth today for people in the future?

Yes. We have a responsibility to people in the future. Why should they suffer because we are too lazy or greedy to look after the Earth?

No. We can do what we like. People can sort out any problems later.

What do YOU think?

It's your right

How do children's rights help young people?

Do you enjoy going to school? In countries such as the UK and Australia, all children are allowed to have an education – it is their **right**. **Laws** help people to know their rights and the right way to behave with other people.

Newsflash

In some countries, children are not properly protected. The **charity** Amnesty International has told the Tamil Tiger rebels (a group of people in Sri Lanka who have been fighting against their government) that they should stop using children as soldiers. Amnesty International is a worldwide organization that protects human rights. They say some of the Tamil Tiger soldiers are as young as fourteen – and that they should be returned home to their families.

Children's rights

The United Nations **Convention** on the Rights of the Child is an agreement about children's rights. It spells out what children's needs are, and what is fair for all children – no matter who they are or where they live. Apart from many other rights, children have the right to:

◎ have a name
◎ have a home
◎ go to school
◎ be healthy
◎ play
◎ be safe.

In many countries, the law says that everyone has the right to equal treatment at school and at work – whether they are male or female, disabled or of a different race. ◑

Talk time

What is the difference between wants and needs?

Maribel: There are lots of things we all want – sweets, games, toys, books, CDs and stuff!

ali: Yeah! And clothes, too. Though I suppose we need clothes, as well as want them.

Tyrone: But we don't really need the expensive stuff – like designer trainers!

Lauren: We need food and water...

ali: So – there's a difference between things we want and things we need.

Tyrone: Definitely. And we should all have the right to have what we need.

Lauren: Even if we can't have everything we want.

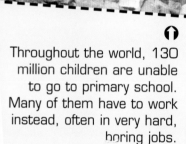

Throughout the world, 130 million children are unable to go to primary school. Many of them have to work instead, often in very hard, boring jobs.

Children's wrongs

Sometimes, children's rights are not respected. People get it wrong. In some **developing countries**, children live in very poor conditions. They may not have a proper home, healthy food or even clean water. Children may have to work instead of going to school.

THINK IT THROUGH

If you have rights, should you have responsibilities, too?

Yes. It's only fair. For example, if you have the right to be safe, you should also have the responsibility not to hurt anybody else.

No. It's up to the law to look after everyone's rights – not me.

What do YOU think?

Everyone is special

What is the right way to treat other people?

One of the most important things in our lives is the way we are treated and the way we treat other people. Everyone is different, and there will always be some challenges as we learn how to be with them. We can get it right or get it wrong.

One of a kind

Look around you. Do you see anyone who is the same as you? No? That is because you are one of a kind! Every person in the world is unique – and everyone is special. We should all be treated just the same, no matter what we look like, where we come from, what our religion is or whether we have a disability.

Top thoughts

'Racism is hurtful and cruel, and no one should have to put up with it.'

Ian Wright,
UK footballer

We are all different – and that's exactly what makes life so interesting!

Discrimination

Discrimination means treating others differently or unfairly because they are not the same as you. There are **laws** against discrimination in many countries, including the UK and Australia. Racism is a form of discrimination against people of a different race or **culture**. Rightly, racism is **illegal**.

In their shoes

It helps you to treat other people well if you can put yourself in their shoes. If you are white, for example, imagine what it would be like to live in a country with mainly black people. How would you feel different? How would you like to be treated? Treating others with kindness and respect is always the right thing to do.

Talk time

How can people learn to treat others well?

ali: You need to remember that everyone has as much right to be here as you have.

Tyrone: Yeah, no matter what colour they are, or whether they have a disability or whatever.

Lauren: It's wrong to make fun of people.

Maribel: Yes – how would you feel if someone made fun of you? It's not fair.

Tyrone: Anyway, even though someone might seem different, there are always things you have in common, too.

ali: Yeah, like football! You just have to find out what they're really like by talking to them.

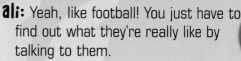

THINK IT THROUGH

Is it a good idea to have awards for children who speak up for what is right?

Yes. Doing the right thing is really important. Making friends with someone who is unpopular can be brave, too.

No. The important thing is being brave physically – like saving someone's life. The rest is only words.

What do YOU think?

How can we help the world with our choices about right or wrong?

Fact Flash

In 2001–02, Oxfam spent nearly £115 million to help people in need all over the world.

Top thoughts

'Helping people in need is a good and essential part of my life.'

Diana, Princess of Wales (1961–97)

We can all make the world a better place – in little ways as well as big. It is simply a question of stopping to think about what we do, and always trying to make the right choices.

The right way

You really can make a difference to the world – in little ways, every day! We all live alongside other people – at home and school, and in our community. By helping and getting on with them, you can make everyone's life much happier. By taking care of property as well as people – for example, by putting litter in bins – you can help to make the world a more pleasant place to live in. And by looking after the **environment** – by **recycling**, for example – you can protect the Earth for people in the future.

Helping out

No matter where you live, you can make a difference to the world by helping **charities** that support other people, animals or the environment. You can help them to raise or collect money, or you can help in other ways, too. There are many charities to choose from, such as Oxfam, which works to help people who are poor or suffering, or World Wide Fund for Nature (WWF), which protects wildlife.

Walking to school, rather than driving, protects the environment, keeps you fit and is fun!

THINK IT THROUGH

Is it OK to just 'do your own thing' in life?

Yes. What I do is up to me. No one can tell me what to do. I'm free to live my own life just as I want.

No. Every single thing I do affects somebody somewhere in some way – so I have to think about that, too.

What do YOU think?

Glossary

charity organization that helps people in need and relies on money that is given to it by the public

consequences results of a person's actions

convention formal agreement between countries to follow the same laws

cosmetics make-up products, such as eye shadow and lipstick

councillor member of a local council, who works on behalf of people in the community

court place for deciding whether or not a person is guilty of committing a crime

culture things that people do and believe in a particular community or country

developing countries countries that are poor with few industries, hospitals and schools

environment our surroundings and the world we live in

extinct dying out completely, so that there are none left

fundraising when people collect money for something or someone in the community, for example, by doing a sponsored walk

illegal against the law

judge person in charge of a court

law rule or set of rules that a whole community or country has to follow

magistrate person with no formal legal training, who is given the authority to enforce the law in magistrates' courts.

local council place where decisions are made about a community

moral when someone does something that is right and fair

mosque place of worship for Muslims

offender person who commits a crime

pollution when harmful substances damage air, land and water

recycle re-use something, either by making something new from it, or by giving it away

right something that is fair and that you can expect

school council group of students who help to make decisions about school issues

vandalism damaging public or private property on purpose

vegetarian person who chooses not to eat meat

volunteer to give up your time freely

Check it out

You can find out more about some of the topics covered in this book by checking out the following books and websites.

Books

Bullying – Why Does It Happen?, Sarah Medina (Heinemann Library, 2004)

The Environment: What's the Problem?, Sarah Medina (Heinemann Library, 2004)

Viewpoints: A Green World?, Nicola Baird (Franklin Watts, 2001)

Rules and Laws: What Are They For?, Sarah Medina (Heinemann Library, 2004)

What Do You Know About Racism?, P. Sanders and S. Myers (Franklin Watts, 2000)

Charity websites

Amnesty International (UK): www.amnesty.org.uk
(Australia): www.amnesty.org.au

Animals Australia: www.animalsaustralia.org

Cystic Fibrosis Trust (UK): www.cftrust.org.uk
(Australia): cysticfibrosisaustralia.org.au

Greenpeace (UK): www.greenpeace.org.uk
(Australia): www.greenpeace.org.au

Oxfam (UK): www.oxfam.org.uk
(Australia): www.caa.org.au

RSPCA (UK): www.rspca.org.uk
(Australia): www.rspca.org.au

World Wide Fund for Nature (UK): www.wwf.org.uk
(Australia): www.wwf.org.au

Other organizations

Crimestoppers (UK): tel. 0800 555 111;
(Australia): tel.1800 333 000

United Nations Pachamama website:
www.grida.no/geo2000/pacha/index.htm

Index